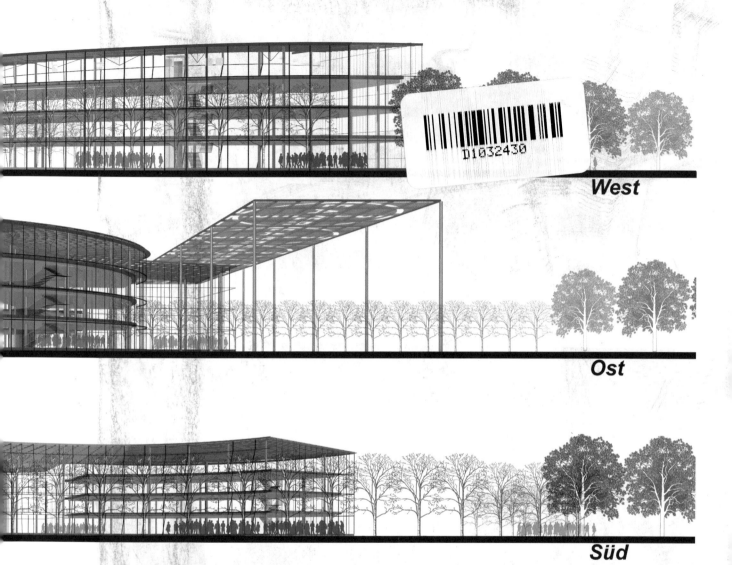

West

Ost

Süd

Nord

Bayer
Konzernzentrale
Headquarters

Werner Blaser

BAYER
KONZERNZENTRALE
HEADQUARTERS

HELMUT JAHN
WERNER SOBEK
MATTHIAS SCHULER

Birkhäuser – Publishers for Architecture
Basel · Boston · Berlin

Translation from German into English: Adam Blauhut, Berlin
Translation of Helmut Jahn's Introduction from English into German: Jutta Amri, Trier

A CIP catalogue record for this book is available from the Library of
Congress, Washington D.C., USA.

Bibliographic information published by Die Deutsche Bibliothek
Die Deutsche Bibliothek lists this publication in the Deutsche Nationalbibliografie; detailed
bibliographic data is available in the internet at http://dnb.ddb.de.

© 2003 Birkhäuser – Publishers for Architecture, P.O. Box 133, CH-4010 Basel, Switzerland.
Member of the BertelsmannSpringer Publishing Group

Printed on acid-free paper produced from chlorine-free pulp. TCF ∞

Layout: Werner Blaser and Keith H. Palmer
Litho and typography: Photolitho Sturm AG, Muttenz

Printed in Germany

ISBN 3-7643-7003-3

9 8 7 6 5 4 3 2 1   http://www.birkhauser.ch

Inhaltsverzeichnis   Contents

Geleitwort

Kann ein Gebäude Sinnbild einer Unternehmensphilosophie sein? Ist es möglich, die funktionalen Anforderungen mit ästhetischen Ansprüchen zu vereinen?

Die architektonische Leistung von Helmut Jahn dokumentiert das eindeutige «Ja» auf diese Fragen, die am Anfang unserer Überlegungen zum Bau einer neuen Bayer-Konzernzentrale standen. Kernaussagen unserer Unternehmensphilosophie – Transparenz, Weltoffenheit und Zukunftsorientierung – hat Helmut Jahn mit den Mitteln der Architektur übersetzt. Seine «Sprache» ist jedem Betrachter verständlich: Große doppelwandige Glasflächen sowie der Kunststoff Makrolon schaffen kristalline Klarheit. Die sich zu einer Parklandschaft hin öffnende Halb-Ellipse des Komplexes vermittelt gemeinsam mit der weitläufigen, hellen Vorfahrt sowie der großzügigen Eingangshalle das Gefühl von Weite und Offenheit. Die Verwendung moderner Baumaterialien und eine außergewöhnliche Formgebung symbolisieren das vorwärtsgerichtete Denken und Handeln des «global player» Bayer.

Ohne Zweifel ist die neue Konzernzentrale ein High-Tech-Produkt. Dennoch ist es gelungen, die Aspekte des Umweltschutzes zu integrieren. Nicht nur, dass das Innere des Gebäudes den Blick auf den angrenzenden Park freigibt und sich dessen Natur in der Glasfassade widerspiegelt. Auch die Technik dokumentiert das Umweltbewusstsein des Unternehmens. Ein Beispiel dafür ist die neuartige Klimakonzeption des Hauses: Innovativ und ressourcenschonend dient die gläserne Doppelfassade der Temperierung und Belüftung des viergeschossigen Komplexes.

Die zukunftsweisende Verbindung aus Gestaltung und Technik bietet den Mitarbeiterinnen und Mitarbeitern in der Konzernzentrale Arbeitsbedingungen in außergewöhnlicher Arbeitsatmosphäre. Durch diese bewahrheitet sich ein mehr als 2 500 Jahre altes Zitat des griechischen Redners Antiphon, der feststellte: «Die Umgebung, in der sich der Mensch den größten Teil des Tages aufhält, bestimmt seinen Charakter.»

Offenheit und Stil des neuen Gebäudes inspirieren sowohl die hier beschäftigten Menschen als auch die Besucher. Weder dem Blick noch den Gedanken sind Mauern gesetzt. Die charakteristische Transparenz des Hauses steht für die Nähe zu unseren Kunden, unseren Mitarbeitern, unseren Aktionären und der Gesellschaft.

Bayer AG

Werner Wenning
Vorsitzender des Vorstandes

Foreword

Can a building be a symbol of a corporate philosophy? Is it possible to combine functional requirements with aesthetic aspirations?

Helmut Jahn's architectural achievement has provided an unequivocal "yes" to these questions, which essentially formed the starting point for our plans to build the new Bayer Group headquarters. Using the architectural means available to him, Helmut Jahn has succeeded in translating the core statements of our corporate philosophy – transparency, openness and orientation to the future – into a visible language. It is a language that is comprehensible to anyone looking at the building. The extensive areas of twin-walled glass and Makrolon plastic symbolize crystal-clear transparency. The half-oval-shaped building opens on to the park, which, together with the wide, bright drive and the spacious reception hall, underscores the message of space and openness. The use of modern construction materials and unique design features reflect Bayer's cosmopolitan, future-oriented attitude as a global player.

Although the new Group headquarters is unquestionably a high-tech product, it nevertheless successfully integrates important environmental protection aspects. Not only does the inside of the building afford an uninterrupted view of the adjacent park, reflecting the natural landscape in the glass facade, but the engineering also bears witness to the company's environmental awareness. The innovative air-conditioning system is one example: the resource-saving "twin-shell" facade acts as a natural skin, adapting to external weather conditions to control the temperature and ventilate the four-story building.

The cutting edge combination of design and technology provides the building's occupants with ideal working conditions in an unusual atmosphere. It also proves the truth of a more than 2,500-year-old quote from the Greek orator, Antiphon, who said: "People's characters are determined by the place where they spend the majority of their day."

The openness and style of the new building are an inspiration both to those who work here and to visitors. There are no solid walls to block the view or stifle the ideas of the people inside. The distinctive transparency of the building is a symbol of Bayer's closeness to our customers, our employees, our shareholders and society.

Bayer AG

Werner Wenning
Chairman of the Board of Management

Bayer Konzernzentrale: Einführung von Helmut Jahn

Konzept:

Im Jahr 1998 schrieb die Bayer AG einen beschränkten internationalen Wettbewerb für die Planung des Baus ihrer neuen Konzernzentrale aus. Das vorhandene Hochhaus war in großem Maße renovierungs- und umbaubedürftig und sollte durch ein kleineres, effizienteres Gebäude im anliegenden Park ersetzt werden. In diesem Gebäude sollte nur das Top Management mit dessen Mitarbeitern und den entsprechenden Sitzungs-, Konferenz- und Verpflegungseinrichtungen beherbergt werden. Unser Entwurf wurde auf Grund der innovativen architektonischen und ingenieurtechnischen Entwurfskonzepte ausgewählt.

Städtebaulich fügt sich die halbelliptische Gebäudeform in den südlich anliegenden nach dem Firmengründer benannten Carl-Duisberg-Park ein, darin stellt eine große Brunnenanlage das Bayer Markenzeichen dar. Im Norden betont eine langgestreckte Pergola die Linearität des Straßenraums und bildet einen Gegenpol zur alten Konzernverwaltung. Die verglaste Eingangshalle stellt das verbindende Glied zwischen dem öffentlichen Bereich und dem privaten Park her.

Funktion:

Alle Funktionsbereiche sind von der Eingangshalle aus erreichbar. Diese ist Mittelpunkt und Symbol für die zukunftsgerichtete und weltoffene Haltung des Konzerns. Die Plankonfigurationen sind flexibel und ermöglichen die Anordnung von Fluren mit ein- oder doppelseitigen Raumanordnungen für die verschiedenen Funktionsbereiche. Die Führungskräfte sitzen in der obersten Etage und genießen großzügigere Raumhöhen und natürliches Tageslicht von oben. Im Untergeschoss befinden sich Parkplätze und Versorgungseinrichtungen.

Konstruktion:

Der Baukörper ist als Stahlbetontragwerk mit wenigen aussteifenden Querwänden ausgeführt. Die Sichtbetondecken der Büroetagen werden mit Hilfe eines Rohrnetzwerkes thermisch aktiviert und somit zu einem Bestandteil des Klimasystems. Weiterhin sind die Deckenunterseiten mit breiten Vouten ausgebildet. Einerseits spart man hierdurch Gewicht und andererseits dienen diese als Reflektoren für die Beleuchtung der Büros mit eigens dafür entworfenen Leuchten.

Die Dachkonstruktion besteht aus einem Stahlraster und geschweißten Stahlhohlprofilen, welche auf Stahlstützen aufgelagert sind. Die fast entmaterialisierten Glaswände in der Eingangshalle werden von vertikal gespannten Stahlseilen gehalten, welche dauerhaft mit Spiralfedern vorgespannt sind. Die Befestigung der großformatigen Glasscheiben erfolgt mit Klemmen, was eine minimierte Bemessung des Glases erlaubt. Das Dachraster über der Eingangshalle wird von schlanken, konisch geformten Stützen punktuell getragen. Diese sowie alle anderen lastabtragenden Komponenten des Gebäudes beeinflussen dessen klaren architektonischen Charakter durch den Wegfall unnötiger Werkstoffe, durch nüchterne Materialverwendung und das optimierte Design der Komponenten hinsichtlich des Kraftflusses.

Bayer Headquarters: Introduction by Helmut Jahn

Concept:

In 1998 Bayer held a limited international competition for their new Headquarters Building. The existing high-rise was in need of major repair, remodeling and replacement by a smaller and more efficient building in the adjacent park, housing only top management with its staff, meeting, conference and dining facilities. Our project was chosen based on its innovative architectural and engineering concepts proposed.

Urbanistically the semi-elliptical shape engages the Bayer Park to the south where a memorial to Bayer's founder Carl Duisberg goes back to the company's roots. In the court of the building Bayer's logo is rendered as a large fountain. To the north a long Pergola reinforces the linearity of the adjacent street and confronts the original Headquarters. The glazed entry hall becomes the connective link between the public precinct and the private park.

Function:

All functions are accessible from the central hall. It becomes the center and representation of Bayer's progressive corporate culture. Plan configurations are flexible and allow for single or double-loaded corridors for the different functions. Executive functions on the top floor enjoy increased room heights and top lighting. Parking and services are in a basement level.

Structure:

The structure of the building consists of a concrete skeleton with few sheer walls. The exposed concrete slabs of the office floors are thermally activated by means of a network of pipes and become a component of the heating and cooling system. The underside of the ceiling has been structured with wide coffers. They save weight and act as reflectors for the office lighting with specially designed light fixtures.

The roof structure above the top office floor is a two-way mesh grid and welded hollow steel profiles, supported on steel columns. The nearly de-materialized glass walls in the entry hall are held by vertically spanning steel cables, which are permanently pre-stressed by means of springs. The large panes of glass are fixed to the cables by clamps which allows a more minimal structural dimensioning of the glass. The roof grid above the entry hall is carried on point supports by slender, cone-shaped columns. They influence its architectural character significantly by the deletion of unnecessary materials, by their honest use, and by the optimized design of the components according to force flow.

The structure of the Pergola was originally envisioned to be of carbonfiber, to push for more advanced technology and materials in building construction, like in cars or sailboats. Higher costs forced us to go back to a steel structure, which is covered by polycarbonate louvers with integral dichromatic film. This results in changing colors and their projection. The Pergola is thus a part of the landscape concept and a display of advanced technical materials.

Enclosure:

The facade is adaptable and switchable. It controls its environment by design and not through additional technical equipment. Natural ventilation, daylight with its connected solar energy

Die Konstruktion der Pergola sollte ursprünglich aus Karbonfaser sein, um fortschrittliche Technologien und Materialien, wie sie im Segelboot- oder Automobilbau verwendet werden, in das Gebäude einzubinden. Die hohen Kosten veranlassten uns jedoch dazu, zu einer Stahlkonstruktion zurückzukehren. Das Dach der Pergola besteht aus einem Raster aus Polycarbonatplatten mit integrierten dichroitischen Folien. Dies führt zu wechselnden Licht- und Farbenspielen. Die Pergola bildet somit Teil des landschaftlichen Gesamtkonzeptes und wird zum Aushängeschild der innovativen technischen Materialien.

Gebäudehülle:

Die Fassade ist anpassungsfähig und regulierbar. Sie beherrscht ihre Umgebung durch Design und nicht durch zusätzliche technische Ausrüstung. Das Konzept liegt in natürlicher Belüftung und Tageslicht in Verbindung mit Sonnenenergie sowie deren elektronische Steuerung. Es wird so zum Vermittler zwischen den äußeren Bedingungen und der gewünschten Behaglichkeit der Nutzer im Innenbereich. Der Komfort ist maximiert, die technische Ausrüstung minimiert. Das Ziel ist die Annäherung an die wunderbare biologische Anpassungsfähigkeit der menschlichen Haut.

Um die natürlichen Resourcen zu maximieren und die technische Ausrüstung auf ein Mindestmaß zu reduzieren, entschieden wir uns für eine zweischalige Fassade. Die voll verglasten inneren und äußeren Schalen ermöglichen die natürliche Belüftung, sind Wind-, Regen-, und Lärmschutz und erlauben die Platzierung des Sonnenschutzes hinter der Außenschale. Die Klimaregulierung erfolgt durch Luftansaugung aus dem gesteuerten Luftraum zwischen den Schalen durch die Fenster oder durch spezielle Öffnungen am Deckenrand. Die Luft wird durch die dort befindlichen Konvektoren je nach Bedarf erhitzt oder abgekühlt und von dort aus nach dem Quellluftprinzip verteilt. Dieses System unterstützt den Hauptheiz- und Kühlkreislauf des in den gevouteten Betondecken integrierten Rohrsystems.

Die Südfassade ist schuppenartig nach außen geneigt arrangiert, um eine bessere natürliche Luftzirkulation bei hohen Außentemperaturen zu ermöglichen. Regulierbare horizontale Klappen am Überstand der Scheiben ermöglichen die zentrale Steuerung. Die Außenschale der Nordfassade ist durchgehend gerade. An den Wandenden und in der Halle sorgen Edelstahlgewebe für Sonnenschutz und bewahren die Transparenz des Gebäudes.

Das Dach ist mit einem zellulären Paneelsystem gedeckt. Es dient als Dacheindeckung, Dämmung, Lärmschutz, Belüftung und es lässt den Einfall von Tageslicht genau dort zu, wo es erwünscht ist. Über der Eingangshalle befinden sich Glaszellen mit spezieller Beschichtung zur Steuerung der solaren Wärmeenergie.

Energie/Komfort:

Durch die Integration dieser architektonischen und technischen Strategien entsteht ein Gebäude mit geringem Energieverbrauch und maximalem Komfort.

Der erhöhte Wärmeschutz der Gebäudehülle reduziert den erwarteten Wärmebedarf auf 35 kWh/m²a, was etwa 30 % unter den Anforderungen der neuen deutschen Energiesparverordnung liegt. Der Sonnenschutz ist durch die Screen-Fassade geschützt. Er ist damit höchst zuverlässig und erlaubt die Kühllasten bis auf die internen Werte für Menschen und

and their intelligent control are the main strategies. They mediate between the external conditions and the desired internal comfort of the users. Comfort is maximized and technical equipment is reduced. The goal is to approximate with the facade the wonderful adaptability of the biological human skin.

In order to maximize the natural resources and minimize technical equipment, we opted for a "twin-shell" facade. The fully glazed outer and inner glass-shells enable natural ventilation, protect from noise, rain and wind and allow for placement of shades behind the outer shells. For conditioning, air is taken from the controlled airspace between the shells through the windows or a special detail at the slab edge and heated or cooled by a convector in the raised floor and distributed from there using the displacement principle. This system supports the basic heating and cooling through the integrated piping system in the coffered exposed concrete slabs.

At the south-face the facade is shingled to allow for better natural airflow at hot outside temperatures. Operable flaps at the gaps of the shingles allow for central control. The outer shell of the north-face is straight. At the end walls and the hall fixed stainless steel mesh provides sun protection and preserves transparency.

The roof is covered with a cellular panel-system. It acts as roofing, insulation, acoustic barrier, accommodates local ventilation and admits daylight, where desired. Above the entry hall glass cells were used with special fritting to control the solar gains.

Energy/Comfort:

The integration of these architectural and engineering strategies results in a building which uses less energy and maximizes comfort.

The increased thermal protection of the building enclosure reduces the expected heating demand to 35 kWh/m²a, which is about 30% below the requirements of the new German energy code. The shading device is protected by the screen facade. It acts as a very reliable sun and glare protection and allows dropping the thermal loads down to the internal gains by people and equipment. The artificial lighting is controlled depending on the natural illumination through daylight. The minimized loads can be handled through the concrete slabs or the metal cooling panels on the fourth floor which are activated either by a night ventilation or the integrated plastic piping, connected to the ground water from the nearby river, which provides a natural cooling source with temperatures of 15–18 °C. This cooling source could not be used in a typical air conditioning system, which demands 6–8 °C cooling temperatures. By covering the cooling and basic heating demand by the thermal radiation of the tempered ceiling surface the thermal user comfort is maximized.

To ensure the fresh air supply for the offices in periods with the facade closed to the vertical and horizontal buffer space – due to cold and hot outside temperatures and demands for privacy or sound protection – the facade-convectors are connected to "sound protected" air intake openings. These decentralized air-intake units allow preconditioning and filtering the fresh air, streaming in from the facade buffer into the offices as displacement ventilation. Through this concept, individual temperature control for heating and cooling and individual

Geräte zu senken. Die künstliche Beleuchtung wird je nach Grad des natürlichen Tageslichteinfalls gesteuert. Die minimierten Belastungen können über die Betonplatten oder die metallischen Kühlplatten auf der vierten Etage reguliert werden. Diese Kühlplatten werden entweder durch nächtliche Belüftung oder durch integrierte Plastikrohre aktiviert, die mit dem Grundwasser des nahe gelegenen Flusses verbunden sind, welcher mit Temperaturen von 15 – 18 °C als natürliche Kältequelle dient.

Durch die Deckung des Hauptkühl- und Heizbedarfs über Wärmestrahlung der temperierten Deckenflächen, wird die thermische Behaglichkeit des Benutzers maximiert.

Damit die Frischluftzufuhr der Büros auch in Zeiten gesichert ist, in denen die Fassade an den vertikalen und horizontalen Pufferzonen geschlossen ist, etwa bei zu heißen oder zu kalten Außentemperaturen und beim Bedarf nach Privatsphäre oder Lärmschutz, sind die Fassadenkonvektoren an lärmgeschützte Ansaugöffnungen gekoppelt. Diese dezentralisierten Ansaugöffnungen ermöglichen eine Vorklimatisierung und Filterung der Frischluft, welche von den Fassadenpuffern in die Büros als steuerbare Belüftung einströmt.

Dieses Konzept ermöglicht auf einfache Weise die individuelle Temperaturregelung für Aufheizung, Kühlung und Frischluftzufuhr. Ein Abluftsystem sammelt die verbrauchte Luft aus jedem Raum und wird zur Klimaregulierung der unbeheizten Eingangshalle benutzt.

Im Vergleich zu Gebäuden in Standardbauweise ermöglicht dieses innovative und integrierte Energiekonzept die Reduzierung des Energieverbrauchs aus fossilen Rohstoffen um 50%, und trotzdem erhält es oder erhöht sogar den Grad der Behaglichkeit. Der Heizbedarf wird bis auf 35 kWh/m²a reduziert, Kühlung erfolgt über natürliche Quellen und 2 kWh/m²a elektrische Pumpenkraft. Die künstliche Beleuchtung wird schätzungsweise auf 11 kWh/m²a verringert, und der Belüftungsaufwand dürfte 8 kWh/m²a Energieverbrauch nicht übersteigen. Der gesamte Primärenergiebedarf für Heizung, Kühlung, Belüftung und Beleuchtung sollte sich hiermit unter dem Wert von 120 kWh/m²a einpendeln.

control of the fresh airflow can be easily realized. A controlled exhaust system collects the used air room by room and uses it for basic conditioning of the unheated entrance hall.

The innovative and integrated energy concept allows the requirement for energy from fossil fuels to be reduced by more than 50% compared to a standard building, but keep or increase the comfort levels. Heating will be reduced to 35 kWh/m²a, cooling is covered by natural sources and 2 kWh/m²a pump electricity, artificial lighting is minimized to an estimated 11 kWh/m²a and ventilation energy should not exceed 8 kWh/m²a electricity. This should allow the total primary energy demand for heating, cooling, ventilation and lighting to be kept below 120 kWh PE/m²a.

Außenraum

Idee und Gestalt

Das formale und ästhetische Erscheinungsbild der neuen Konzernzentrale von Bayer ist eine Halbellipse, die sich dem Carl-Duisberg-Park zuordnet. Es ist von einer Transparenz geprägt, die im bewussten Gegensatz zu den Altbauten des Konzerns steht und damit symbolhaft und zukunftsweisend für Bayer im 21. Jahrhundert ist. Dieser Neubau zeigt sich schlicht und selbstverständlich, dabei ohne falsche Bescheidenheit. Er ist kein Gebäude des Zurück-blickens in die Geschichte der Architektur, sondern ein Bau, der die Möglichkeiten der Gegen-wart intelligent und verantwortungsbewusst für die Zukunft anwendet.

Das Gebäude liegt ganz im Park. Die Porte Cochère setzt die Geradlinigkeit der Kaiser-Wilhelm-Allee fort und schafft den Übergang zum Gebäude. Der Bogen des Baukörpers hält den Blick auf das Kasino frei. Der Parkplatz für 68 Fahrzeuge und die Zufahrt zur Tiefgarage sind in die Parklandschaft und den verbleibenden Keller des ehemaligen Hochhauses inte-griert. Der Eingang liegt direkt gegenüber dem monumentalen Eingang des alten Haupt-verwaltungsgebäudes. Das Bauwerk bezieht sich auf das bestehende Kasino, ohne es zu bedrängen. Die Porte Cochère ist eine Stahlleichtbaukonstruktion mit modularen, halbtrans-parenten Makrolon-Elementen.

Wegen der Bedeutung des Carl-Duisberg-Parks für Bayer, dessen Mitarbeiter und die Gemeinde Leverkusen, war die landschaftliche Situierung des Neubaus besonders wichtig. Durch die Bogenform des Baukörpers verbleibt genügend Parkland, so dass der Zugang und die Sichtverbindung zum Park offen bleiben. Der zu schützende Baumbestand bleibt beste-hen. An der Kaiser-Wilhelm-Allee wird die Platanenallee fortgesetzt. Die landschaftliche Gestaltung des Parks wird nach Abbruch des Hochhauses bis an die Kaiser-Wilhelm-Allee her-angeführt. Auf der Südseite des Gebäudes ist in einer Vertiefung eine runde Wasserfläche angelegt, in der das Bayer-Kreuz als «Wasserskulptur» dargestellt ist. Die Buchstaben sind Edelstahl-Wehre, über die das Wasser abfließt.

Exterior Space

Form and Idea

The formal and aesthetic design of the new Bayer Group headquarters is based on an open half oval that embraces Carl Duisberg Park. It is characterized by a transparency that stands in marked contrast to the company's older buildings and makes a symbolic, forward-looking gesture at the start of the 21st century. The new building is straightforward and natural in appearance and devoid of any false modesty. It does not dwell on architectural history but intelligently and responsibly exploits present opportunities for the future.

The building is situated entirely in the park. The Pergola reinforces the linearity of Kaiser-Wilhelm-Allee while creating a transitional space in front of the building. The curved shape of the headquarters preserves the view of the Kasino, Bayer's staff restaurant and hotel facility. A 68-car parking lot and the drive leading to the underground car park have been integrated into the park landscape and the old tower's basement. The entrance lies directly across from the monumental entrance to the old administration building. The headquarters engages the Kasino without encroaching on its space. The Pergola is a lightweight steel structure with modular, semi-transparent Macrolon elements.

Carl Duisberg Park is an important landmark for the Bayer Group, its employees and the community of Leverkusen, and it was essential that the new headquarters blend well into the landscape. The curved shape of the building leaves sufficient space to ensure access and views of the park. Tree stocks have remained intact, and the avenue of sycamores is continued on Kaiser-Wilhelm-Allee. After the old tower is demolished, the landscaping will extend right up to Kaiser-Wilhelm-Allee. In a depression on the southern side of the building, there is a water sculpture of the Bayer cross. The letters are stainless steel weirs over which the water flows.

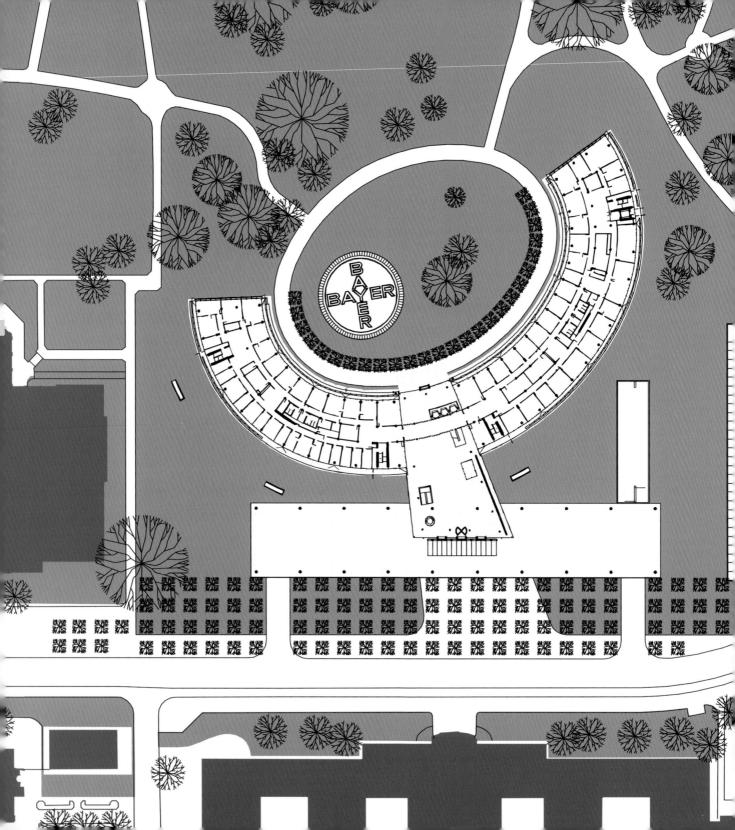

Fassade

Material und Konstruktion

Gegenwärtige Ingenieur-Kunst und Technologie zwingen herkömmliche Materialien und Systeme in Grenzen. Das Hauptinteresse gilt nicht dem High-Tech, sondern der Verbesserung der Leistung des Gebäudes. Die Form ist minimal und einprägsam. Durch die Integration von Material und Konstruktion wird in der neuen Konzernzentrale eine bewusste Komplexität erreicht. Wie in einem Diagramm ist diese Organisation ablesbar.

Das Gebäude ist als Stahlbetontragwerk konzipiert. Die Decken sind dünne Stahlbetonplatten, unterstützt von runden Stahlbetonstützen und aussteifenden Stahlbetonkernen. Dadurch wurde eine effiziente und bauzeitsparende Konstruktion erzielt. Die Porte Cochère, die Einganshalle, die Verbindungsbrücken und die Dachkonstruktion über dem dritten Obergeschoss sind als Stahlleichtbaukonstruktionen ausgebildet. Das Dach ist ein stützender, isotropischer Mesh-Grid: er besteht aus geschweißten Stahlhohlprofilen, auf welche die Dachzellen montiert werden.

Die zweischalige Fassade ermöglicht die natürliche Belüftung der Büros, wann immer es die Außentemperatur erlaubt. Die äußere Haut gibt Schutz vor Regen, Wind und Lärm und ermöglicht im Zwischenraum vor der inneren Haut das Hängen der Sonnenschutz-Jalousien. Die geschoßhohen Glaswände optimieren die Tageslichtnutzung. Sonnenschutz und Licht werden automatisch gesteuert und kontrolliert. Vor allem im Sommer und Winter sorgt ein dezentrales Quellluftsystem mit individuellen Kühlungs- und Heizungselementen entlang der Fassade für ausreichenden Komfort. Die Grundkonditionierung wird durch eine in die Betondecken integrierte Bauteilheizung/-kühlung erreicht. Die zweischalige Fassade funktioniert wie eine natürliche Haut, indem sie sich den äußeren klimatischen Bedingungen anpasst und mit Hilfe minimaler Gebäudetechnik die optimalen und gewünschten Innenraumbedingungen schafft. Dadurch werden beträchtliche Energieeinsparungen gegenüber einschaligen Fassaden erzielt.

Die Idee, dass die Hülle eines Gebäudes unter Nutzung von Tageslicht und Solarenergie ihr eigenes Klima moduliert und so für natürliche Belüftung sorgt, wurden bis jetzt in dieser Form noch nicht realisiert. So können wir in einer zunehmend technisierten Welt dennoch auf unsere natürlichen Bedürfnisse eingehen. Das Resultat sind Gebäude mit High Technology und Low Energy.

Facade

Material and Structure
Current engineering trends and state-of-the-art technology are pushing traditional materials and systems to their limits. The focus is not on high tech, but on improving building performance. Forms are minimal and striking. In its new headquarters, Bayer has achieved a deliberate complexity through the integration of material and structure. The structure allows the organization within to be read like a diagram.

The building has been designed as a reinforced concrete skeleton. The floors are made of thin reinforced concrete slabs, supported by circular concrete columns and concrete bracing cores. This design made it possible to construct the headquarters quickly and efficiently. The Pergola, the entrance hall, the connecting "bridges" and the roof over the fourth floor are all lightweight steel structures. The roof is a supporting, isotropic mesh grid. It consists of welded hollow steel sections on which the roof panels are mounted.

The "twin-shell" facade allows for natural ventilation of the offices, exterior temperature permitting. The outer shell protects against rain, wind and noise, and sunshades can be placed in front of the inner shell. The floor-to-ceiling glass walls make optimal use of daylight, with sunshades and illumination controlled automatically. In the middle of summer and the dead of winter, a decentralized displacement ventilation system ensures sufficient comfort through individual cooling and heating elements along the facade. The basic conditioning is achieved by integral pipes in the concrete slabs for heating and cooling. The "twin-shell" facade functions like a natural skin by adapting to exterior climatic conditions and creating the optimal interior conditions using minimal building services technology. This results in considerable energy savings as compared to single-shell facades.

A building facade that modulates its own climate using daylight and solar energy has never been executed in this form. The facade enables human beings to satisfy their natural needs in an increasingly technologized world. The resulting building represents high technology and low energy.

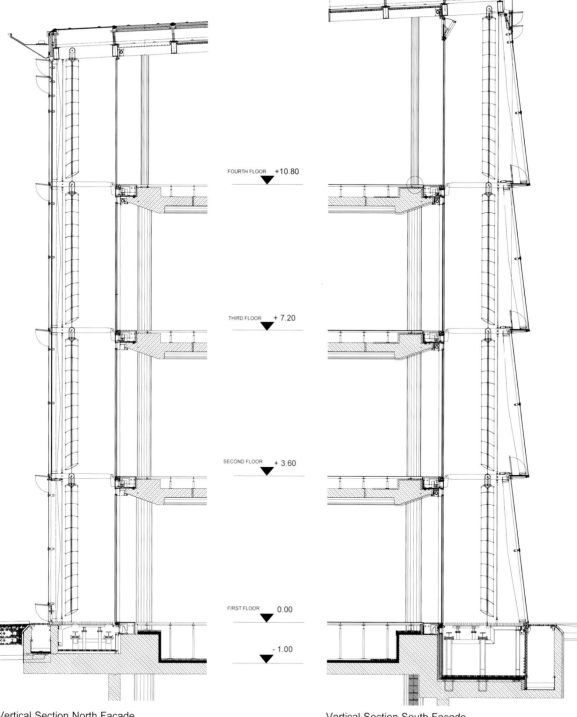

FOURTH FLOOR   +10.80 ▼

THIRD FLOOR   + 7.20 ▼

SECOND FLOOR   + 3.60 ▼

FIRST FLOOR   0.00 ▼

− 1.00 ▼

Vertical Section North Facade

Vertical Section South Facade

0   1   2   3   4 m

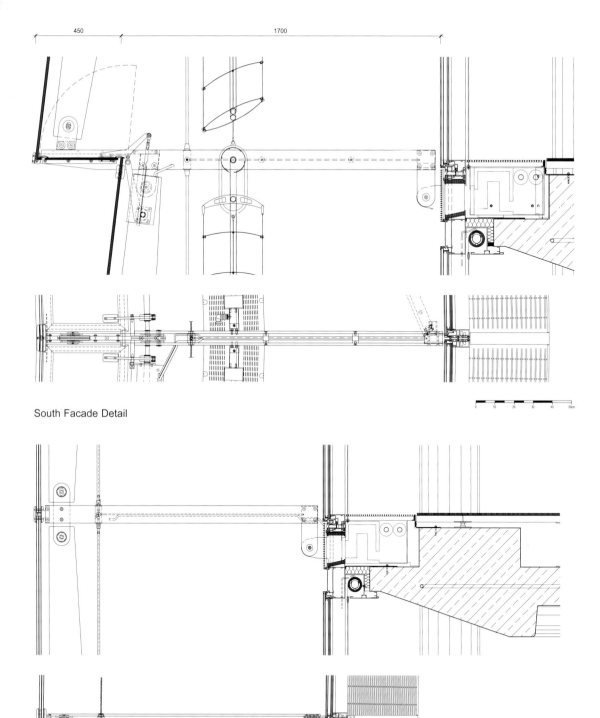

450   1700

South Facade Detail

0   10   20   30   40   50cm

North Facade Detail

0   10   20   30   40   50cm

Innenraum

Proportion und Raum

Die Einganshalle unterschneidet die Porte Cochère. Die Erschließung der drei Obergeschosse von der Eingangshalle durch Glasaufzüge und eine Freitreppe ist klar und erlebnisreich. Der Carl-Duisberg-Park ist von der Halle, den Aufzügen, der Treppe und den Verbindungsbrücken der Bürotrakte gut sichtbar. Der Baukörper selbst ist 19,5 m breit. In der Mittelzone sind Nebenräume ohne Tageslichtbedarf und technische Räume untergebracht. Das Raumprogramm enthält Bereiche für Empfang, Vorstand, Aufsichtsrat, Konferenzen, Gästebewirting, Küche, Senior Management, Assistenten, Hausverwaltung, Chauffeure, Nebennutzungen und Tiefgarage.

Das erste Obergeschoss beherbergt das Senior Management mit Räumen für leitende Angestellte und Assistenten sowie Besprechungs- und Konferenzzimmer. Das zweite Obergeschoss bietet eine Kombination von Senior-Management-Büros mit Mittelzone im Ostflügel und Konferenz- und Besprechungsfunktionen mit Mittelgang im Westflügel. Im dritten Obergeschoss, der sogenannten Vorstandsetage, wird die Möglichkeit genutzt, gefiltertes Tageslicht vom Dach in die Räume zu bringen. Dies macht vor allem die breite Mittelzone zum lichtdurchlässigen Raum für Zugang, Empfang und tiefere Büroräume. Die Lage im obersten Geschoss und der spezielle Raum- und architektonische Charakter schaffen eine besondere Umgebung für die Vorstandsfunktionen. Die besondere Aufenthaltsqualität wird durch Terrassen gesteigert, die von den Büros begehbar sind und von denen sich der Carl-Duisberg-Park überblicken lässt.

Das Dach vollendet die Fassadenhülle. Über dem Stahlraster sind auswechselbare Zellen angeordnet: geschlossen oder transparent mit unterschiedlichem Sonnenschutz und Lichtlenkung, äußere Hitzeabsorption, Schallregulierung, Lüftung und innere Hitzeabsorption.

Interior Worlds

Proportion and Space

The entrance hall overlaps the Pergola. From the hall, visitors have access to the three upper stories via glass elevators and an open stair in a clearly laid-out, vibrant space. Carl Duisburg Park is visible from the entrance hall, the elevators, the stairway, the connecting bridges and office wings. The building itself is 19.5 meters wide. The middle area accommodates technical facilities and side rooms that have no need of natural daylight. The spatial concept provides reception areas and offices for executives, managerial staff, office workers, property management staff, chauffeurs, ancillary uses and the human resources department.

The second floor houses senior management and office workers, as well as meeting and conference facilities. In the east wing of the third floor there are executive suites arranged around a central zone, while the west wing features conference and meeting facilities branching off a central corridor. On the fourth floor – the so-called Board Floor – daylight filters through the roof, flooding the wide central zone used for access routes and secretariats with light. The open reception areas afford a view of the building's surroundings. This location on the top floor, combined with the special character of the space and the architecture, creates an attractive setting for board activities. This special quality is enhanced by terraces that are accessed directly from the offices and offer a view of Carl Duisberg Park.

The roof completes the building envelope and is equipped with adaptive cells that perform different functions, e.g. solar protection, light channeling, exterior heat absorption, acoustic damping, ventilation and interior heat absorption.

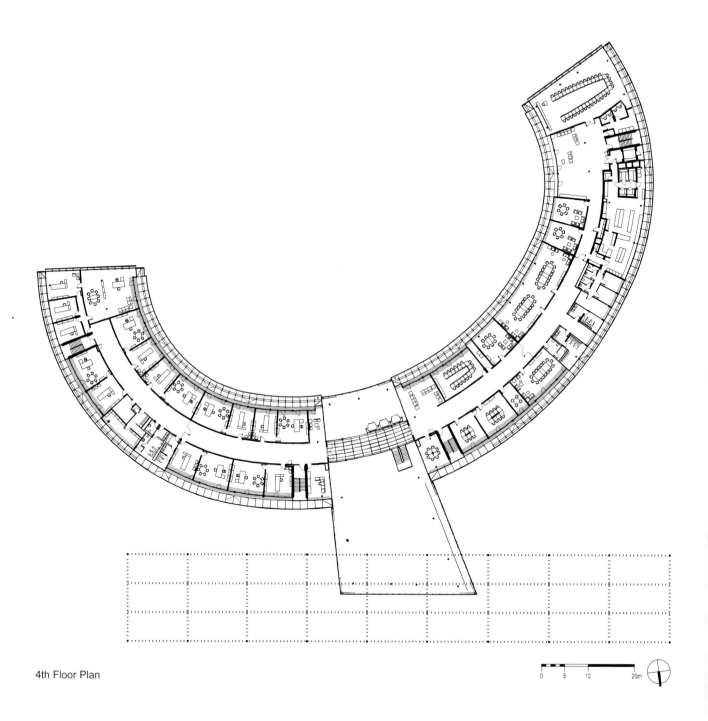

4th Floor Plan

0   5   10   20m

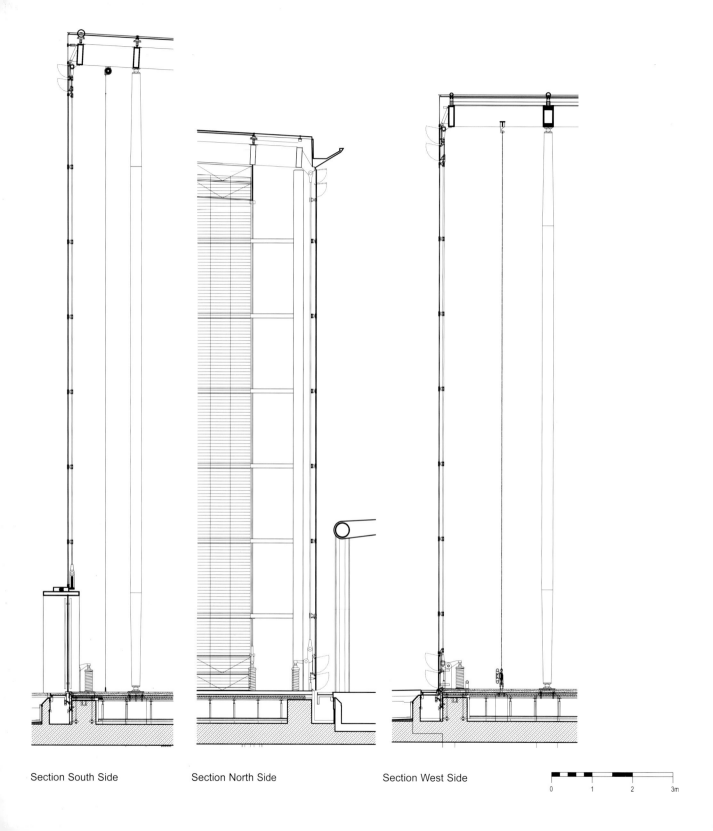

Section South Side   Section North Side   Section West Side

0   1   2   3m

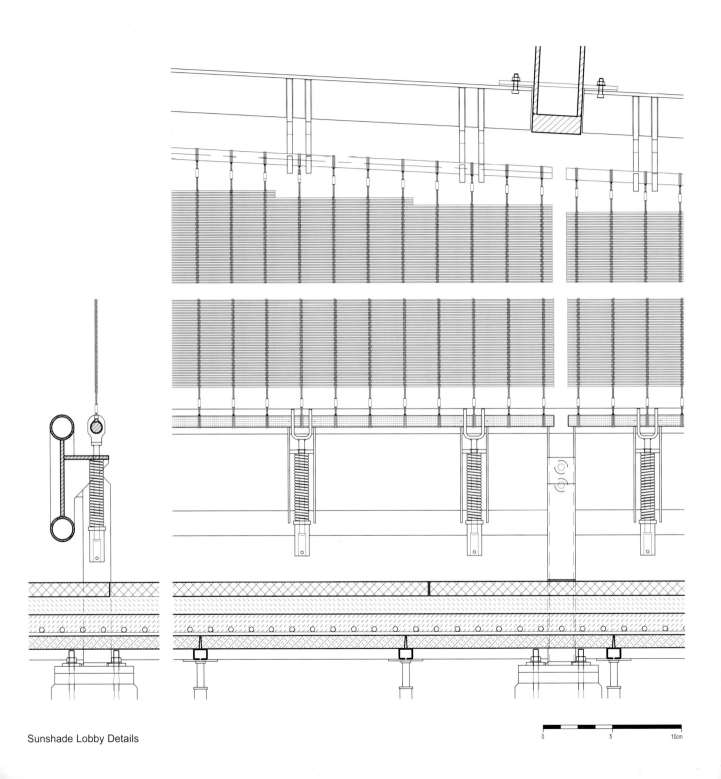

Sunshade Lobby Details

0   5   10cm

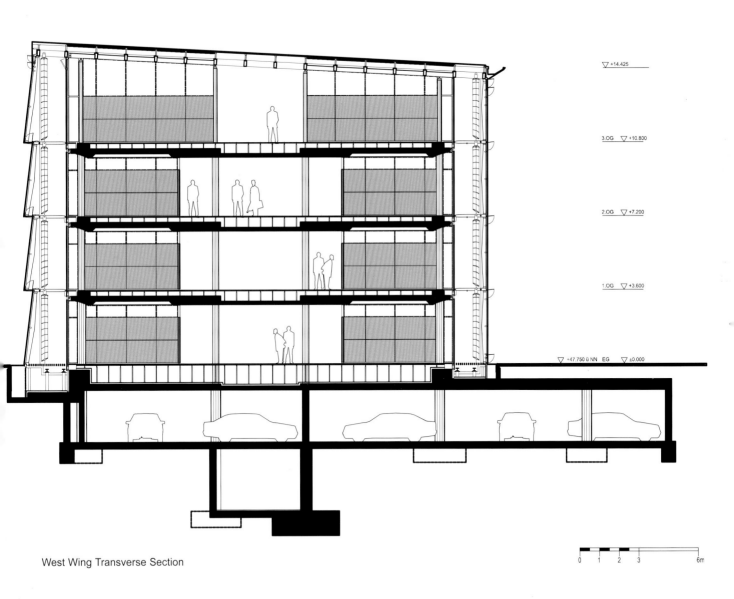

▽ +14.425

3.OG ▽ +10.800

2.OG ▽ +7.200

1.OG ▽ +3.600

▽ +47.750 ü NN EG ▽ ±0.000

West Wing Transverse Section

0 1 2 3   6m

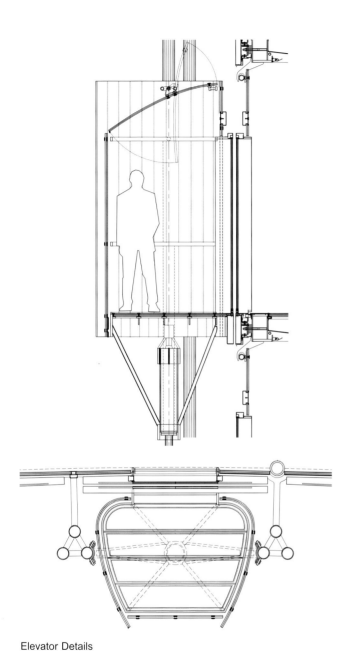

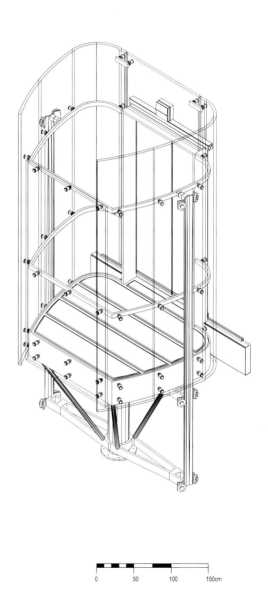

Elevator Details

0   50   100   150cm

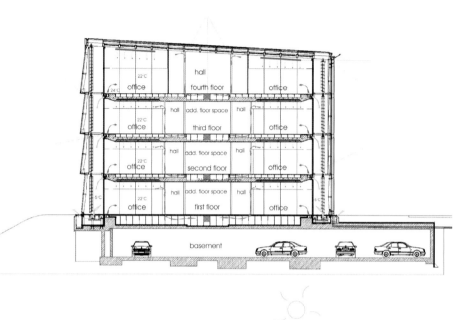

hall
22°C office | fourth floor | office
24°C

hall | add. floor space | hall
22°C office | third floor | office

hall | add. floor space | hall
22°C office | second floor | office

5°C | hall | add. floor space | hall | 5°C
22°C office | first floor | office

basement

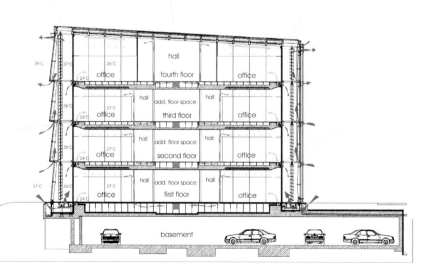

hall
39°C | 37°C | 26°C office | fourth floor | office
24°C

hall | add. floor space | hall
36°C | 27°C office | third floor | office
24°C

hall | add. floor space | hall
35°C | 27°C office | second floor | office
24°C

37°C | 34°C | hall | add. floor space | hall
27°C office | first floor | office
24°C

basement

Baukunst und Ingenieurkunst als Impuls

Wir sprechen von Baukunst und stellen ihr die Ingenieurkunst als ebenbürtigen Partner gegenüber. Dies umso mehr, als im zeitgenössischen Bauen die Gebäudeenergie einen hohen Stellenwert einnimmt. Im Begriff Engineering wird das Ingenieurwesen und die Gebäudetechnizität zusammengefasst. Das Denken des Architekten wird im Engineering in ein wirkungsvolles Gesamtkonzept umgesetzt. Unabdingbare Voraussetzung hierfür ist eine grundlegende Kooperation zwischen Architekten, Bauingenieuren und Gebäudetechnikern.

Seit 1994 wurde der deutsch-amerikanische Architekt Helmut Jahn (Chicago) auf die progressiven Arbeiten der Tragwerkplanung des Stuttgarter Ingenieurbüros von Werner Sobek aufmerksam. Im selben Zeitraum ergaben sich Synergien mit der seit 1992 in Stuttgart arbeitenden Firma Matthias Schulers, Transsolar Energietechnik. Die daraus entstandene, konsequente Zusammenarbeit ist ausführlich dokumentiert in meinem 2002 erschienenen Buch «Architecture Engineering».

Die Außenhaut und die Glastechnologie der neuen Bayer Konzernzentrale gehen auf eine innovative Entwicklung von Werner Sobek und Matthias Schuler zurück. In der Zusammenarbeit mit Helmut Jahn entstand eine ökologisch und ökonomisch sinnvolle Konstruktion, die ein geringes Gewicht aufweist, eine gute Belichtung sichert und Langlebigkeit garantiert.

Architecture and Engineering as Impetus

It seems warranted today to speak of architecture and engineering as equal partners. Energy use has become a key issue in contemporary architecture and the term "engineering" includes building services technology. Through engineering, the architect's ideas are translated into an effective overall concept. For this to be successful, there must be extensive collaboration among architects, engineers and building technicians.

The progressive structural planning work by Werner Sobek's engineering firm in Stuttgart first attracted the attention of the German-American architect Helmut Jahn (Chicago) in 1994. At this time synergies were achieved between Sobek's office and Transsolar Energietechnik, which Matthias Schuler established in Stuttgart in 1992. These synergies formed the basis of the close cooperative relationship between the two companies that I have documented in detail in my book Architecture Engineering (2002).

The exterior shell and glass technologies of the new Bayer Group headquarters are based on an innovative development by Werner Sobek and Matthias Schuler. In cooperation with these two men, Helmut Jahn has designed an environmental, economically viable structure that is lightweight, optimally illuminated and will have a long life.

Präzision und Eleganz

Im Bayer-Werk in Leverkusen hatte der Hochhaus-Klassiker der Fünfziger Jahre von HPP ausgedient. An seiner Stelle empfahl ein internationaler Wettbewerb 1998 das Projekt Helmut Jahns für eine neue Konzernzentrale der Bayer AG zur Ausführung. Jahn nutzte die grundsätzliche Idee der grandiosen Parkanlage und entwickelte ein langgezogenes, gekurvtes Bauwerk mit vier Etagen. Das volltransparente Gebäude erreicht die volle Baumhöhe nicht und hält so den Blick auf den alten Baumbestand aufrecht. Nichts an dem Bau ist überflüssig, wodurch die helle Freundlichkeit der Innenräume noch unterstrichen wird. Die optische Taille der Stahl- und Glasarchitektur vermittelt grazile Eleganz und weckt die Neugierde.

Die Natur mit den ihr innewohnenden Kräften und Gesetzen ist Gewordenes und Gewachsenes. Im Kontrast dazu steht die Architektur als Schöpfung des menschlichen Geistes. Aufgabe des Architekten ist es daher, Natur und Bau zur Synthese zu bringen. Helmut Jahn löste diese Aufgabe in Zusammenarbeit mit Werner Sobek und Matthias Schuler hier im Sinne einer Metamorphose, die von der Volltransparenz des Bauwerkes getragen wird.

Ein Hauch von Sinnlichkeit erfüllt die Innenräume. Er entsteht nicht zuletzt durch die Geste der Nüchternheit und der Leere im Zentrum des Baus. Das Gebäude gleicht einem Baum mit vier breitgewachsenen Ästen, dessen Stamm das hohe Gebäude-Foyer bildet: ein leerer, durchscheinender Kubus, von Norden nach Süden ausgerichtet. Dieses Entrée ist die Grundgestalt des Baus, die zu Interaktionen zwischen Mensch und Natur einlädt. So spricht das Bauwerk alle Sinne an und vermittelt die unverwechselbare Idee des Natürlichen.

Filigrane Stahldetails, wohlgeordnet und -gefügt, tragen zur Stille und Zurückhaltung des Gebäudes bei. Dem Experiment und der Schönheit im Detail sind keine Grenzen gesetzt. So sind etwa die Anschlüsse bei den Stützen an Boden und Decke mit einer dünnen runden Platte auf einer Kugel angeschlossen: So heben sich Tragen und Lasten von der Fläche ab. Wir kennen die Konsolen der alten chinesischen Baumeister, welche – vom Bildhauer bearbeitet – die schlanken, tragenden Holzsäulen auf Sockel stellten. Dieses «Abheben» unten und oben wird in der Konstruktion wiederholt. Die Säule verliert ihre Schwere. Sie wird zur Signatur einer Symbiose aus Statik und Ästhetik. Über das Zweckhafte hinaus vermittelt hier das Tragen eine Präzision und Eleganz, die dem Bau seinen eigenen Zauber verleiht.

Precision and Elegance

HPP's high-rise classic from the 1950s, situated in the Bayer complex in Leverkusen, was outdated, and in 1998 the jury of an international competition recommended replacing it with the design for a new Bayer headquarters by Helmut Jahn. The German-American architect had adopted the basic idea of the grand park and developed a long, curved four-story building. The fully transparent structure preserves the view of the existing trees since it does not rise to their full height. Nothing about the building is superfluous, and the bright, inviting air of the interior space is enhanced by this economy. The optical waist of the glass-and-steel architecture conveys a graceful elegance and awakens the observer's curiosity.

Nature with its inherent forces and laws is the part of our world that has evolved and grown over time. By contrast, architecture is a creation of the human spirit. The mission of architecture is to achieve a synthesis between nature and building. In cooperation with Werner Sobek and Matthias Schuler, Helmut Jahn has fulfilled this goal through a metamorphosis based on the full transparency of the building.

A breath of sensuality fills the interior space, originating in its empty, sober core. The building resembles a tree with four long branches, its trunk formed by the high lobby. This empty, transparent cube, running north to south, encapsulates the basic form of the building and promotes interaction between mankind and nature. This building speaks to the senses, imparting a distinctive idea of what is natural.

Finely wrought steel details, pleasingly arranged and joined together, contribute to the building's composure and reserve. No limits have been placed on experimentation and beautification of detail. The ends of the columns at the ceiling and floor are connected to a thin round plate on a ball, thus "lifting" the load-bearing elements off the frame. The consoles designed by old Chinese architects are well-known: they were fashioned by sculptors and used to support slender wooden columns. This "lifting" at bottom and top recurs in this structure. The columns lose their heaviness. In the structure we discover a symbiosis of structural engineering and aesthetics. Transcending function, the load-bearing columns convey a precision and elegance that lends the building its magic.

Im Team der drei Disziplinen

Zur Elite im Bauwesen, als inspirierende Gestalter unserer Zeit, gehören Helmut Jahn und Werner Sobek. Beide sind in ihren Disziplinen Weltbildner. In der Verknüpfung von Architektur und Engineering wird das Konstruktive sichtbar gemacht. Beide sind Interpreten der Industrialisierung in der wahren Integration von Architektur und Engineering. Ihr hohes denkerisches und künstlerisches Teamwork ist als Kunst in der Architektur- und Ingenieurwissenschaft zu bewerten: der Architekt, ein tiefblickender Analytiker der Skelettbauweise und der transparenten Raumdurchdringung; der Ingenieur, ein folgenreicher Interpret der Leichtbauweise im Bauen mit Stoff und im Bauen mit Licht.

Zum objektivierbaren Anteil von Architektur gehört auch die kreative Gebäudetechnik von Matthias Schuler. Jede architektonische Kreation braucht ihr technisches Gegenspiel, um das innere und äußere Erscheinungsbild unserer Erlebniswelt in weitblickender Verantwortung zu prägen. Der gesamtverantwortliche Anspruch eines Bauwerk liegt in der kreativen Zusammenführung eines ganzheitlichen Konzepts, welches auch die Solartechnik einschließt. Das Technisch-Innovative ist von Anfang an mit dem Gestalterisch-Kreativen vereint und wird in die architektonische Gestalt umgesetzt. Dabei sind zahlreiche funktionale, technische und kommunikative Anforderungen zu berücksichtigen, welche in die vorgestellte Architektur zu transformieren sind.

One Team, Three Disciplines

As inspiring designers and demiurges in their respective fields, Helmut Jahn and Werner Sobek belong to the world's architectural elite. Through the union of architecture and engineering, structure is rendered visible. Both men interpret industrialization through the true integration of architecture and engineering. Their skilled conceptual and artistic teamwork must be viewed as an art form from the perspective of both architectural and engineering sciences. The architect is a profound analyst of skeleton construction and transparent spatial penetration, the engineer an influential interpreter of lightweight construction methods that incorporate materials and light.

Matthias Schuler's creative application of building services technology is the objectifiable aspect of a work of architecture. Every architectural creation requires its technical counterpart to responsibly shape the interior and exterior of our experiential worlds for the future. The responsibility of a building lies in creatively realizing an integrated concept that includes solar technology. From the very start, technology and innovation are united with design and creativity, and from this unity the architectural form is born. Numerous functional, technical and communicational requirements must be fulfilled that are transformed into the envisioned architecture.

Technische Angaben und die am Bau Beteiligten / Technical Data and Names of Persons Involved

Bauherr / Client:	Bayer AG
Architekt / Architect:	**Murphy/Jahn, Inc.** Helmut Jahn, Sam Scaccia, Rainer Schildknecht, John Durbrow, Stephen Kern, Wolfgang Bauer, Alphonso Peluso, Rob Muller, Joachim Schuessler, Barbara Thiel-Fettes, Jan Goetze, Michael Bender
Tragwerks- und Fassadenplanung / Structure and Enclosure:	**Werner Sobek Ingenieure GmbH** Werner Sobek, Norbert Rehle, Frank Tarazi, Agnes Landauer, Dieter Möhrle, Wolfgang Straub, Dietmar Klein IGH Ingenieurgesellschaft Höpfner GmbH
Energieplanung / Energy and Climate:	**Transsolar Energietechnik GmbH** Matthias Schuler, Tobias Fiedler
Heizung, Lüftung, Sanitär / Building Services	**Brandi Consult GmbH** Tibor Rákóczy, Udo Bartz
Landschaftsgestaltung / Landscape Design:	**Peter Walker & Partners** David Walker Wolfgang Roth, Freier Landschaftsarchitekt
Bauphysik und Akustik / Building Physics and Acoustics:	Horstmann + Berger Jürgen Horstmann
Bauleitung / Construction Supervisor:	Heinle, Wischer und Partner Achiel Rombaut, Florian Farr
Lichtplanung / Lighting Design:	Dinnebier-Licht-GmbH Hella Dee, Monika Lohmann
Brunnen / Fountain:	Wolfgang Schrötter
Architekturwettbewerb / Architectural Competition:	04/1998
Fertigstellung / Completion	04/2002
Programm / Program:	Konzernzentrale, Büros für leitende Angestellte und Management, Konferenzräume und Stabsrestaurant, Tiefgarage für 152 Fahrzeuge. Corporate headquarters, executive and managerial offices, conference and staff dining facilities. Underground parking for 152 cars.
Bruttogeschossfläche / Gross floor area	23 000 m²
Fläche oberirdisch / Above ground floor area	16 000 m²
Fläche unterirdisch / Below ground floor area	7000 m²
Typische Geschossfläche / Typical floor area	3300 m²
Gesamtfassadenfläche / Total facade area	6900 m²

Biografische Notizen

Helmut Jahn

Geboren 1940 in Nürnberg. Architekturstudium an der Technischen Hochschule in München, dann am Illinois Institute of Technology in Chicago. Seit 1967 bei C.F. Murphy Associates, wo er 1973 Partner wurde. 1981 wurde das Büro in Murphy/Jahn umbenannt, und 1983 übernahm er das Büro ganz.

Seit über dreißig Jahren verfolge ich den Aufstieg von Helmut Jahn als Architekt, Chefarchitekt und Firmeninhaber. Sein erstes selbständiges Werk, die Auraria Library in Denver, publizierte ich 1977 in «after Mies». Später entstanden die Bücher «Airports» 1991, «Transparenz» 1996 und «Architecture/Engineering» 2002, alle im Birkhäuser Verlag Basel–Boston–Berlin.

Architektur war immer eine Kunst, die Visionen Gestalt gibt. Es gehört zur Architecture-Engineering-Partnerschaft mit realistischen Grundlagen, das Neue leidenschaftlich anzupacken. Insbesondere konnte Helmut Jahn sein Image der «high-tech architecture» durch die Partnerschaft mit den Ingenieuren in ein zeitgemäßes umwandeln, das seiner heutigen Realität entspricht.

Werner Sobek

Geboren 1953 in Aalen (Württemberg). Bauingenieur- und Architekturstudium an der Universität Stuttgart, mit Promotion zum Doktor-Ingenieur. 1991 Gründung seines Ingenieurbüros in Stuttgart und 1995 Professor an der Universität Stuttgart, Leiter des Instituts für leichte Flächentragwerke und des Zentrallabors des konstruktiven Ingenieurbaus. Aus seinem Werk ist 1999 das Buch «Werner Sobek: Art of Engineering/Ingenieur-Kunst» und 2001 die Monografie «R 128» mit Frank Heinlein entstanden.

Matthias Schuler

Geboren 1958 in Stuttgart, Abschluss 1987 als Diplom-Ingenieur an der Universität Stuttgart, danach Assistent am Institut für Thermodynamik und Wärmetechnik. 1992 Gründung der Transsolar GmbH für Klima Engineering in Stuttgart, eines Technologie-Büros für energieeffizientes Bauen und Nutzkomfort in Gebautem.

2001 Gastprofessur an der Harvard University, Department of Architecture.

Im 2003 bei Birkhäuser erscheinenden Band «Transsolar – KlimaEngineering» wird dessen Arbeit ausführlich vorgestellt.

Biographical Notes

Helmut Jahn

Born in Nuremberg in 1940, architectural studies at the Technische Hochschule in Munich and later at the Illinois Institute of Technology in Chicago. Joined C.F. Murphy Associates in 1967, made a partner in 1973. In 1981 the firm was renamed Murphy/Jahn and in 1983 Jahn took control of the business.

I have followed the rise of Helmut Jahn as architect, chief architect and CEO for more than thirty years. His first independent work, the Auraria Library in Denver, was presented in my book After Mies (1977). There followed a series of books on his work, all published by Birkhäuser Verlag (Basel, Boston and Berlin): Airports (1991), Transparency (1996) and Architecture/Engineering (2002).

Architecture has always been an art that lends visions a concrete form. Every architecture/engineering partnership with a foundation in reality must demonstrate a passion for innovation. Through his partnership with engineers, Helmut Jahn has been able to revamp his image as a "high-tech" architect, making it more contemporary and reflective of his current work.

Werner Sobek

Born in Aalen (Württemberg) in 1953, civil engineering and architectural studies at the University of Stuttgart, doctorate in engineering, 1991 establishment of his own engineering firm in Stuttgart, 1995 professorship at the University of Stuttgart, director of the Institut für Leichte Flächentragwerke and the Zentrallabor des Konstruktiven Ingenieurbaus. His work is described in the book Werner Sobek: Art of Engineering/Ingenieur-Kunst (1999) and the monograph R 128, co-authored with Frank Heinlein (2001).

Matthias Schuler

Born in Stuttgart in 1958, master's degree in engineering in 1987 from the University of Stuttgart, lecturer at the Institut für Thermodynamik und Wärmetechnik. In 1992 Schuler founded Transsolar GmbH für Klima Engineering in Stuttgart, a technology company devoted to energy-efficient architecture and utilitarian comfort in buildings.

2001 visiting professorship at the Harvard University, Department of Architecture.

The book Transsolar – KlimaEngineering, which will be published by Birkhäuser in 2003, presents the company's work in detail.

Über den Autor

Werner Blaser, geboren 1924 in Basel, studierte nach einem Praktikum bei Alvar Aalto am Illinois Institute of Technology in Chicago, wo er unter anderem mit Mies van der Rohe in Kontakt trat. In eigenen Entwürfen, zahlreichen Ausstellungen und Architekturpublikationen über Ost-Europa, Japan und China sowie Monografien über seine Lehrmeister Aalto und Mies van der Rohe setzt er sich seit Jahren mit den Fragen und Prinzipien der Architektur auseinander. In Basel führt er ein eigenes Büro für Architektur, Möbeldesign und Publizistik.

About the author

Born in Basel in 1924, Werner Blaser completed his practical training with Alvar Aalto and then continued his studies at the Illinois Institute of Technology in Chicago which brought him into contact with such figures as Mies van der Rohe. Original designs, numerous exhibitions and publications on Eastern Europe, Japan and China, as well as monographs on his mentors Aalto and Mies van der Rohe have, for years, been Blaser's means of confronting and analyzing architectural questions and tenets. Now heading his own firm in Basel, he is active as designer, architect and publicist.

Bücher über die Architekten/Ingenieure von Werner Blaser bei Birkhäuser/
Books available about the architects/engineers by Werner Blaser at Birkhäuser:

Deutsche Post Zentrale/Headquarter. Helmut Jahn – Werner Sobek – Matthias Schuler, 2003
Helmut Jahn – Architecture Engineering. Helmut Jahn – Werner Sobek – Matthias Schuler, 2002
Werner Sobek: Art of Engineering/Ingenieur-Kunst, 1999
R128 by Werner Sobek (Werner Blaser/Frank Heinlein), 2002